COIN COLLECTING for Beginners

Grow a Treasure on Your Desk! The Easy Guide to Start Your Coin Collection. Take Your First Steps Into a Hobby that Can Get You Both Fun and Money

ISAIAH O.D. LYNCH

© **Copyright 2020 by** *Isaiah O.D. Lynch*

All rights reserved.

This document is geared towards providing exact and reliable information with regards to the topic and issue covered. The publication is sold with the idea that the publisher is not required to render accounting, officially permitted, or otherwise, qualified services. If advice is necessary, legal or professional, a practiced individual in the profession should be ordered.

- From a Declaration of Principles which was accepted and approved equally by a Committee of the American Bar Association and a Committee of Publishers and Associations.

In no way is it legal to reproduce, duplicate, or transmit any part of this document in either electronic means or in printed format. Recording of this publication is strictly prohibited and any storage of this document is not allowed unless with written permission from the publisher. All rights reserved.

The information provided herein is stated to be truthful and consistent, in that any liability, in terms of inattention or otherwise, by any usage or abuse of any policies, processes, or directions contained within is the solitary and utter responsibility of the recipient reader. Under no circumstances will any legal responsibility or blame be held against the publisher for any reparation, damages, or monetary loss due to the information herein, either directly or indirectly.

Respective authors own all copyrights not held by the publisher.

The information herein is offered for informational purposes solely, and is universal as so. The presentation of the information is without contract or any type of guarantee assurance.

The trademarks that are used are without any consent, and the publication of the trademark is without permission or backing by the trademark owner. All trademarks and brands within this book are for clarifying purposes only and are the owned by the owners themselves, not affiliated with this document

INTRODUCTION — 8
   What Is Coin Collecting? — 8

CHAPTER ONE - WHY COLLECTING COINS? — 14
   Start Your Collection — 15
   Lincoln Cent Series — 16
   50 States and America The Beautiful Quarters — 19
   Beyond Circulation Coins — 21

CHAPTER 2 - VOCABULARY — 26

CHAPTER 3 - BUILDING A COLLECTION — 34
   A Solitary Activity? — 35
   Collecting And Your Family — 35
      Collecting and Your Spouse — 36
      Collecting and Your Children — 37
   Coin Clubs And Organizations — 40
      Local Clubs — 40
      Regional Clubs — 42
   National Organizations — 44
      Young Numismatists Organizations — 46

Learned Societies 46

CHAPTER 4 - THE VALUE OF THE COIN 48

CHAPTER 5 - HOW AND WHERE TO GET COINS? 54
Where to Get Coins? 55
    Coin Dealers 57
    Online Auctions 59
    Local Coin Shows 61
    National Coin Shows 62
    International Conventions 62
    Other Collectors 63
    The US Mint 64
Investing In Coin Sets 64
Tips For Coin Auctions 65

CHAPTER 6 - COLLECTIBLE COINS 68
Silver Coins 70
Junk Silver 73
Silver Rounds 75
Gold Coins 77

CHAPTER 7 - PRESERVE AND PROTECT THE COLLECTION   **82**

    Mint Coins   84

  Coin Care And Cleaning   84

    Soaking coin   88

  How to Store Your Coins   89

    Collectible Coins in their Cases   91

  Protecting Your Collection From Loss By Fire Or Theft   92

CHAPTER 8 - BUYING COINS   **96**

CHAPTER 9 - MONETIZING YOUR HOBBY   **106**

    Coins Public Auction   107

  The Finer Points Of Selling Your Collection   112

  Wholesale Coin Prices   113

  Two Ways To Sell Your Coin Collection   115

CHAPTER 10 - ANATOMY OF A COIN   **118**

BONUS CHAPTER - BUYING COINS: SAFETY UPDATE   **126**

CONCLUSION   **136**

To G.G. "Cats", Roberto "Bob" Mantelli and Chris "Glue" Merrit

Three of my best friends and fellow coin collectors

INTRODUCTION

What Is Coin Collecting?

Anyone who keeps one or more coins for any reason is coin collecting. Some gather coins as a hobby while others for immediate or long term financial gain. Some people collect to teach their children about math, coins, and money.

Some others collect because they want to invest now but plan on passing the collection down to their heirs. Some save a specific coin type or date because it holds sentimental value (gold, silver, error, foreign, ancient, commemorate, or proof coins, for example). Some collect every major coin made. The list goes on.

Don't let the coin field box you in mentally. There isn't a single person that knows it all, and every collector has a different degree of knowledge. In other words, do not let the vast amount of information overwhelm you. Everyone started at ground zero. We are here on this earth to help each other.

Let's define the term "rare coin." After all, in coin collecting, we hear this term so much. What is a rare coin? Is a rare coin one that has a considerable value attached to it? The word "rare" means uncommon, distinctive, extreme of its kind. A definition of "rare coin" can somehow be a rare coin and may or may not have value. In other words, some coins are very rare and very uncommon, yet do not have much value. Some are very valuable. I will show you why this is.

Coin collectors, on the other hand, typically think in terms of money value when using the term "rare coin." For example, I have seen very uncommon coins, maybe only a few in existence, have no value, and therefore, coin collectors would not consider them rare. The problem with the term "rare coin" is that there is no standard definition; for example, is a coin that is worth $1000 a rare coin or not? If you are interested in buying rare coins, what should you buy? Don't worry, and it will all become clear to you.

Coins that continually go up in value over time and are hard to find and or purchase because they are scarce and, when found, can only be purchased for much more than their face value is probably a good definition for "rare coins." As far as investing and this book is concerned, this is the definition we will use.

Remember, from an economic point of view, a coin is only worth what somebody is willing to pay for it. I have seen a one of a kind coin worth an estimated $100,000 and other coins that have had over 50,000 of them minted, and they sell for $50,000 in very good condition. I am going to show you what coins are considered "rare" and why.

We are going to explore coins and coin collecting in-depth. There are many reasons for this, but the principal one is to help you develop a strong knowledge of your investments to make sensible decisions. As stated before, certain rare coins give a higher rate of return than any other investment class over time. Certain coins, like pre-1933 gold coins, do not make good investments. U.S. Mint bullion coins are often purchased at prices that make it hard for the investor to recoup anything, especially over short periods.

You may have in mind a rather famous (at least in the coin collecting and investing world) chart, that has been around for decades, showing how the stock market returned about 11% and rare coins in high grade about 13%. I want to update these figures using more current data.

The drawn-out thankfulness for great uncommon coins has accomplished returns surpassing those of the significant value files. Thinking back in recent years, uncommon coins have had an exacerbated (IRR) pace of return more noteworthy than 11%, while the DJIA and S&P500 records have become at rates under 7%. Interestingly, rare coins increased slightly in value between 2006 and 2010, while the equity markets went down. We must balance this information with events of the last few years, which have seen the DJIA and S&P500 have extraordinary growth, more than the 7% just mentioned.

But the facts over time are clear: rare coins do very well.

Asset Type	Five-Year Holding Period Returns (1970-2005)			
	Average	Standard Deviation	Sharpe Ratio	Rank
Silver	5.52%	16.83%	-0.03	14
Gold	8.81%	19.28%	0.14	8
Oil	8.70%	15.79%	0.17	6
Homes	6.12%	2.82%	0.02	11
Land	6.17%	6.35%	0.02	12
MSCI World	7.84%	10.97%	0.16	7
S&P	8.14%	9.29%	0.22	4
DJIA	8.15%	8.72%	0.24	3
T-Bill	6.07%	2.54%	0.00	13
DiGenova AU	7.96%	9.12%	0.21	5
DiGenova UNC	9.50%	10.07%	0.34	1
DiGenova Both	9.07%	9.33%	0.32	2
BU Rolls	7.45%	17.60%	0.08	10
Solomon	6.73%	6.73%	0.10	9

An interesting chart reflecting a long term study shows how well rare coins do over the years. The study compares rare coins to many other asset classes. Silvano DiGenova is one of the world's greatest coin authorities, and his rare coin tracking data is based on real sales. Note how his UNC (uncirculated) returns for 35 years rank above all other investment classes on the chart.

The fourth line from the bottom (DiGenova UNC) shows a return of 9.5%. Compare this to silver, gold, oil, and the others. Notice the ranking of from 1 to 14 on the right-hand column. The top two rankings are for coins. Again, keep in mind the years for the study, which ended in 2005. The world is different now. The stock market is very robust, but coin returns still rank high. You can see why coin information is so critical. Let's start at the beginning, and we will work our way up.

CHAPTER ONE

-

WHY COLLECTING COINS?

For the vast majority of people, collecting is about the adventure of the pursuit and the fulfillment when you, at last, complete a set following quite a while of chasing for that last small coin. To get the greatest out of your pastime, set yourself explicit goals for coins you'd like to get your hands on and begin looking.

A lot of pastimes require a huge money effort, but not this one. In fact, gathering coins is virtually cost-free. Of course while you proceed in your path you will want to add that particular piece to your collection, and then you will probably want tos spend some money. But for that time you will also have learned the real value of coins and how to buy them in such a way that the money you spend won't be wasted. In fact you will end up considering your pastime money as an investment

Start Your Collection

Starting your coin collection is simple. The best news is it doesn't have to cost anything!

All you need to do is simply reach into your pants pockets or purse. Many coin collectors get their start in the hobby exactly this way. They'll find a coin in change that looks different or is unusually bright. It sparks an interest that leads to finding more about that particular coin.

There's little risk. Beginning your first coin collection from the change you receive every day doesn't cost you anything. I find collecting from circulation to be challenging. Much of the coinage that passes through our hands tends to be worn. So finding a well-preserved coin in pocket change is a welcome surprise.

If starting your coin collection turns out to be something that's not for you, just put the coins back into circulation by spending them.

Lincoln Cent Series

By far, the most popular coins to collect are Lincoln Cents. We receive them in change nearly every day. Much older date Lincoln Cents are still in circulation.

The U.S. started minting Lincoln Cents in 1909, and through 7 major design changes over the years, it is still in production today. Many collectors have made a career of just collecting and studying Lincoln Cents.

Lincoln Wheat-Back series cents were produced from 1909 to 1958. Probably the most famous of these coins is the 1909-S VDB. The "VDB" are the initials of the designer, Victor David Brenner, and are found near the bottom rim on the reverse of the coins.

People were so incensed by the size of the initials that they demanded they be removed. Production was halted, the design changed, and the initials were removed from the coins. Brenner's initials wouldn't reappear on the coin again until 1918, where you'll find them today, on the lower part of Lincoln's shoulder on the obverse of the coin.

Memorial reverse Lincoln cents were introduced in 1959. The obverse of the cents remained the same with Lincoln's bust featured. This design, with minor changes over the years, remained in production until 2008. In 1982 the coins went through a transition from 95% copper to copper-coated zinc. Interesting note: Lincoln Memorial cents arc the only coin produced by the U.S. Mint to feature the same person on both the obverse and reverse.

Look closely at the center of the Reverse side, and you'll find Lincoln in the chair.

The year 2009 was a grand year for Lincoln cent fans. To celebrate the 200th anniversary of President Lincoln's birth, four different reverse designs of the coins were released during the year that depicted President Lincoln's life. The response to these coins' release was similar to the public's response to the overwhelming 1909 cent. Coin collectors and everyday folks stood in lines to receive them. Fewer than 2.4 billion coins total for circulation were minted of the four reverse designs. I know 2.4 billion sounds like a lot, but in the previous year's mintages of cents, it's a small number. How often do you find them in pocket change?

For 2010 the U.S. Mint again released a new reverse version, the Shield reverse, which is still in production today. While it's not the most popular design of Lincoln cents released, it is still popular to find and collect in Mint State condition.

Within the more than 100-year production of the Lincoln, cents are many varieties and error coins collected. Each one is a challenge to the dedicated Lincoln cent collector. I recently had a conversation with a friend who had just completed a full set of Lincoln Wheat cents. He was wondering what to start next. I suggested he might want to consider collecting known error coins. After a few days of thinking about it, he decided that's a great way to extend his collection and increase its value.

50 States and America The Beautiful Quarters

The 50 States Quarter Series was released for circulation in 1999 and quickly became a favorite with collectors. Each year five new reverse designs were released that celebrated a different state. During those ten years, slightly more than 34.8 billion 50 States Quarters were produced. In addition to the regular circulation coins, special silver Quarter Proofs were created especially for collectors. Several

varieties and error coins have been discovered over the years, making completing a set more of a challenge.

These coins are perhaps most responsible for starting new coin collectors on their journey to a great coin collection than any other coins in the last two decades.

The challenge is to create a coin collection of all 50 States Quarters from just what is found in circulation! It can be done, I've done it, and you can, too. It does take some time and a little patience, but it's a great project that can be taken up by the whole family. Get one of the special 50 State Quarters folders to keep your coins in. They're inexpensive and protect your coins, too.

Following up on the 50 States Quarters Series's great success, the U.S. Mint is now releasing the America The Beautiful Quarters series. These quarters feature the nation's National Parks and other national sites. Five designs are being released each year for a total of 56 different coins for the series.

Beyond Circulation Coins

The coin collector getting started today has many options beyond collecting coins from circulation. The U.S. Mint produces sets each year of the coins released for circulation. One of my favorite sets is the Uncirculated Sets that contain one coin of each denomination from each mint where it is produced.

There are also the Proof Sets that are released yearly. Proof coins are specially produced for coin collectors and are minted separately from coins intended for circulation.

Stepping it up a bit, the Presidential $1 coin might be a good series to begin with. To commemorate past Presidents in 2007, the U.S Mint began issuing coins with images of the Presidents on the obverse, the heads side of the coin, beginning with Presidents Washington, Adams, Jefferson, and Madison. Four more coins are released each year with the next four presidents in the order they served.

Again there is little risk if you decide to quit collecting coins, since they can be sent right back into circulation by simply spending them.

You might decide instead of the above coins to start your coin collection with Wheat Pennies, Buffalo Nickels or Roosevelt Dimes. Remember, it's your coin collection, so go for the coins that interest you the most.

Start saving your pocket or purse change. Go through it regularly and save out the coins your interested in. It could be 50 States Quarters, Roosevelt Dimes, Lincoln Memorial Cents, or whatever coin you find the most interesting. It helps to narrow your focus and collect only one series at a time.

Once you've accumulated some coins, purchase an inexpensive folder to store and protect your coins.

Continue to educate yourself about your coins. Now is the time to start locating the books with the in-depth knowledge of the coins you're collecting.

As your collection grows, you may find yourself unable to find the coins you're after in your regular pocket change. Now is the time to visit your local bank, purchase a few rolls of coins, and go through them.

Now is also a good time to add an inexpensive magnifying glass or coin loupe so you can begin examining the details of coins as you sort through them to find the best. You'll also begin learning the "Art" of grading coins in the best way possible - experience!

Most of these coins in circulated condition are inexpensive and can be added to your collection without breaking the bank. Just because coins aren't expensive doesn't mean they won't add up to a significant collection.

As a beginning coin collector, it's best to start with more inexpensive circulated coins to gain experience and knowledge. After you've gained some experience, you'll be better equipped to start looking at more expensive and scarcer coins.

That's not to say you can't start your first collection by acquiring very expensive coins. You're certainly welcome to do that, and coin dealers will thank you for the business. The problem with starting that way? Your mistakes are going to be very expensive.

Don't make mistakes, you say? I don't know of any coin collectors who are honest about it that can't tell you some stories about the coins they should never have bought.

I've kept most of those coins in a special jar. Then, whenever I get antsy to buy a coin I know doesn't fit my collecting goals, I pull out that jar and am reminded why I might want to reconsider buying a problem coin.

You're going to make mistakes. It's part of the hobby. You will come across coins that you'll just believe you have to have and will die if you don't buy it. Those are the coins you want to be wary of.

No matter where you start, remember, it's your coin collection. Collect the coins you want, enjoy the search, educate yourself, involve your kids, and have fun!

CHAPTER 2

-

VOCABULARY

Learning coin collectors' terms/language will help you communicate easily with dealers, other numismatics, and coin collection enthusiasts. The following are some common numismatic terms with their meanings. Get in the know.

- **ANA** (*American Numismatic Association*): the biggest numismatic association for mint piece authorities and those keen on studying cash and its set of experiences

- **About Good** (*AG*): a flawed coin that shows substantial wear. The most reduced evaluation allocated to a coin
- **About Uncirculated** (*AU*): a flowed coin that shows just a limited quantity of wear on the high area(s) of the coin's plan, notwithstanding conceivable contact marks (pack marks). AU is the most noteworthy evaluation relegated to a circled coin
- **Bag Marks**: little scratches or scratches showing up on an, in any case, uncirculated coin brought about by contact with different coins in a mint's unique canvas pack
- **Bid/Ask**: the offer cost is when a seller will pay for collectible coins. Ask cost is the value a merchant will acknowledge for the coin utilizing the spot cost as a source of perspective (see spread definition beneath)
- **Brilliant Uncirculated**: an uncirculated coin has some mint gloss with no wear marks, yet some contact marks are available in at least one coin territory. Generally connected with the lower Mint State evaluations of MS-60 to MS-62.

- **Bullion Coin**: a penny whose significance varies atop the inbuilt valuation of the treasured metallic this one comprises
- **Certified Coin**: a coin that has been reviewed, ensured, and encased in a sealed plastic cover (a.k.a. "slabbed") by one of the perceived reviewing administrations (ANACS, NGC, PCGS, and so on)
- **Choice Uncirculated**: a term commonly used to depict a coin reviewed MS-63, which means some contact marks are available.
- **Clad Coin**: a coin with a center of one metal and an external layer of another metal. Utilized by the U.S. Mint for circled coins starting in 1965
- **Coin Grading**: the way toward deciding how high or low a coin ought to be evaluated, considering wear checks and sack marks, among different elements
- **Commemorative Coin**: a coin delivered to perceive/commend an individual or function
- **Counterfeit Coin**: the multiplication or changing of a coin by somebody other than the authentic guarantor

- **Die**: the metal shape that is utilized to strike/produce a coin
- **Enormously Fine** (*EF* or *XF*): an enclosed penny allocation where the coinage has bright attire altogether the great areas. Though, the intricacies are however piercing
- **Face Value**: the money related worth relegated and stepped on a coin (can be not the same as the real worth is attached to the estimation of the metal it contains)
- **Fineness Or Fine**: The valuable metal level in a coin is comparative with all the metals that make up the coin. For example, a fineness of .900 implies that 90% of the coin is silver and the rest composite
- **Fine Weight**: the genuine load of the silver contained in silver coins (rather than the gross weight, which incorporates the heaviness of the apparent multitude of coin's metals)
- **Fine** (*F*): an assignment of coin evaluating just underneath Very Fine (VF) where the coin has more than the reasonable wear of a VF coin. The plan shows sensible detail.

- **Gem Uncirculated**: an uncirculated coin with few contacts denotes may not be noticeable to the unaided eye. Typically used to depict a coin evaluated MS-65
- **Good (G)**: an assignment of coin evaluating where the coin has critical wear. However, the primary figures are as yet noticeable yet with extraordinary detail misfortune. The second-most minimal evaluation
- **Gram**: in the decimal standard, this is the fundamental unit of weight (31.1033 grams approaches one Troy ounce)
- **Intrinsic Value**: the genuine estimation of the valuable metal (i.e. silver or gold) inside a coin dependent on the current spot cost
- **Legal Tender**: a coin (or money) which an administration or other public financial authority pronounces to be worthy as a mode of trade, can be utilized in the release of obligations
- **Luster**: the sheen or brightness of a newly printed coin brought about by the high weight applied when the coin is struck

- **Market Value**: the going cost of a coin on the open market (which might be equivalent to its inherent worth or more prominent)
- **Mint Mark**: a letter image on a coin that recognizes where it was stamped
- **Mint State**: used to portray a coin that has, for no reason, remained gushed and took not at all garb inscriptions. Mint conditions list beginning 60 throughout 70.
- **NGC** (*Numismatic Guaranty Corporation*): a few of the premier currency studying and validation establishments
- **Numismatic Coin**: a denomination whose value can be determined by the absence, condition, strike, and request with a little accentuation on the estimation of the metal.
- **Obverse**: the frontage of a coin containing the fundamental picture, likewise alluded to as the "heads" sideways
- **PCGS** (*Professional Coin Grading Service*): one of the chief organizations which review and confirms coins

- **Perfect Uncirculated**: undispersed penny that takes stay calculated MS-70, contemplating the " remarkable currency " (partaking not at all flaws).
- **Planchet**: the clear (or coin plate) on which the kick the bucket engraves a coin's plan
- **Premium**: the sum over the spot value that the merchant charges coins so they can get a benefit and stay in business
- **Proof**: a coin created by uncommonly arranged bites the dust utilizing exceptional striking strategies bringing about a serious extent of detail and normally a mirror-like field (the zone encompassing the fundamental image(s)). Verification currencies are made explicitly for gatherers, not implied for course, and not permitted to interact with different coins at the mint
- **Proof Set**: a set comprising one proof coin of every category given by a mint for a particular year.
- **Reverse**: the side inverse the front, alluded to as the "tails' side
- **Spot Price**: the current cost at which coins are utilized to set up purchasing and selling costs (see

offer/inquire). sometimes mentioned as the money cost

- **Spread**: the distinction between the purchasing cost and the approaching cost for a coin
- **Uncirculated**: a coin in new condition (as the mint has given it) that has not been set into dissemination
- **Very Fine** (*VF*): an assignment of coin evaluating where the coin has light to direct even wear on the high regions of the coin yet much detail
- **Very Good** (*VG*): the assignment for a coin that shows extensive wear with the primary highlights clear yet with a fairly straightened appearance
- **Wear Marks**: denotes that show up on the high zones of the front and opposite of a coin because of the coin's course

CHAPTER 3

-

BUILDING A COLLECTION

People who are not involved in coin collecting often view the pastime as a solitary hobby, that is, something for the "closet collector." Uninitiated, no collectors view the collector as a quiet, private individual who strictly assembles a museum-quality collection for his pleasure, likely not sharing his hobby with anyone else. This stereotype is not always accurate!

A Solitary Activity?

There are no reliable statistics to prove that most coin collectors are either introverts or extroverts and perhaps many fit this description of an introvert. Still, there are social aspects to the hobby, and these social aspects can be quite exciting.

Among coin collectors have been such luminaries as Queen Elizabeth II of England, U.S. President John Quincy Adams, Francis Cardinal Spellman, and actor Buddy Ebsen. It could be argued that these well-known people would likely be considered to be extroverts. In more distant history, coin collectors have included such well-known persons as Julius Caesar, Lorenzo de' Medici, and King Louis XIV of France. The social aspects of coin collecting are what you make of them!

Collecting And Your Family

Coin collecting can truly be a family affair. It's a great idea to involve your spouse, and also your children, in your hobby. Here's why.

Collecting and Your Spouse

There are many "widows" of active collectors. These spouses are pleased to see that their partner has a productive hobby but allows the collector to keep the collecting activities to themselves. These nonparticipants in this all-encompassing interest of their spouses are not unlike football widows and other sports fans, but coin collecting is not a seasonal sport.

Some collectors may prefer this privacy, but where possible, it is a great idea to share the hobby with someone you love. There are several good reasons to involve your spouse where possible:

- It promotes good relations between the two of you. This is an interest you can share.

- The non participating spouse should know just how much family money the collector is dedicating to the collection and discretionary money.
- Your spouse might someday be burdened with selling off the family collection after the collector dies. Without understanding the collector's hobby, the coins your family collector acquired, and his contacts, this could become a problem.

Collecting and Your Children

Anytime parents can share in an activity that interests their children, this joint participation will benefit the nuclear family. Many parents become involved as coaches or as spectators to the sporting events in which their children participate. Why not involve your children in your coin collecting interests as well?

Just as coin collectors are sometimes referred to as numismatists, children who collect coins are sometimes referred to as young numismatists or simply YNs.

Surveys indicate that people who were introduced to coin collecting as young children often pursue the hobby until adolescence. These same surveys indicate that once these kids become adults, typically with a family and a stable income of their own, they may once more return to coin collecting.

The same care with which it is suggested an adult enter the hobby—slowly and inexpensively until they understand coin collecting more fully—is also the best way to get a child interested in coin collecting. Let them search through pocket change for coins to fill coin albums. They are too young to appreciate proof sets or something similar an adult simply purchases every year for them. Let them do their collecting; don't do it for them.

Another reason to get your kids involved in your coin collecting hobby is that you can't take it with you. If you consider your coin collection to be your legacy, you need to get your kids interested in it now.

It takes more than an appreciation for what someone else has assembled to want to keep it. One of the foremost collections of U.S. coins ever assembled was resold by the collector's children, who had more interest in the value the collection represented than wanting to keep it intact to have something with which to remember their dad. This mentality is not uncommon.

A significant number of collectors hope in their subconscious minds that their coin collections will be retained and expanded upon by their family after they are gone. This may be wishful thinking, but one thing is certain. If you encourage your family to share in your collecting habit, there is a better chance that they will do just that. Too often, the family collector does not share what he is doing with others, yet incredibly this person still hopes his descendants will still want to retain what he views as his legacy.

As a minimum, you should at least educate your family about the value of your collection so that the surviving family may someday sell it for a fair price. Far too often, without a family being participants in a collection's assemblage, the collection will likely languish in a cabinet or drawer for a generation or two until the emotions surrounding the memory of the collector fade into history, or until some unappreciative finder encounters the collection and chooses to use it as handy "found" money that is very spendable at face value regardless of its value to collectors.

Coin Clubs And Organizations

Involving your family in your coin collecting hobby is important, but it is not the only social aspect. Coin collecting is a highly organized hobby. There are clubs to join, learned societies to go to, shows and conventions to attend, and competitive displays.

Local Clubs

There may not necessarily be a coin collectors' club in your town, but there is likely a club nearby somewhere unless you live in a very rural area. The problem isn't necessarily if a club exists, but in how to find it. Most clubs for coin collectors meet monthly or bi-weekly, often in libraries, churches, banks, or other public places.

You can usually find out about a local club through collector friends by attending a local coin show, contacting the chamber of commerce, or contacting a nearby coin dealer.

Readership surveys conducted by a major coin hobby publication indicate that of collectors who consider themselves to be seriously involved in the more social aspects of the hobby. A majority do not travel more than 50 miles from their home or workplace to participate in coin collecting activities.

Local clubs typically have a modest membership that may or may not include some dealers interested in buying and selling coins. Some clubs have meetings at which you have the opportunity to buy, sell, or trade, while other clubs may want only show and tell rather than commercial activity at their meetings. Some local clubs have their hobby publications, too. If no club exists near you, why not start your own?

There may also be a local coin club for children who collect. Sometimes these are clubs that meet after school, while other times, they may be a local club division for adults. Check with local schools for the whereabouts of these organizations.

Regional Clubs

Many states including California (California Numismatic Association), Pennsylvania (Pennsylvania Association of Numismatists), Florida (Florida United Numismatists), and others have statewide organizations for individuals, local clubs, and commercial coin dealers to belong. These statewide organizations typically have a large annual convention at which they hold their business meetings and conduct educational forums, facilitate buying and selling, hold banquets, and more. Some of these organizations also have their hobby publications worth reading.

There are some even larger regional organizations, one of which is the Central States Numismatic Society. Such organizations draw an audience of both members and nonmembers from a larger geographic area that wants to attend their coin show events.

An organization encompassing this large geographic area also has the luxury of holding their conventions at different locations each time they meet. This can be advantageous for the collector who doesn't want to travel too far from home and second for the collector who wants to contact collectors and dealers from a different region from where he lives. This allows obtaining additional merchandise not necessarily available more locally.

Regional coin collecting organizations sometimes simply encompass a larger geographic area to draw their membership than local clubs. In contrast, others are umbrella groups to which local clubs can belong.

National Organizations

In several countries in which coin collecting is particularly popular, there are national coin collector organizations. These include Belgium, Canada, Great Britain, and Japan. In the United States, the national organization is the American Numismatic Association (ANA).

There are many advantages to belonging to a national organization. For example, ANA membership includes a subscription to the monthly magazine called The Numismatist, access to borrowing books by mail from its extensive library, connecting with other collectors with similar interests, opportunities to buy special insurance to cover the value of your coin collections, and participation in the organization on many different levels.

The ANA holds two week-long conventions every year. The location of these conventions changes, which is good for collectors because the convention will be reasonably close to where the collectors live at one time or another. ANA conventions are worth attending.

A mammoth gathering of professional dealers sells everything from inexpensive coins to some of the world's most valuable coins and banknotes, educational forums, specialty and regional club meetings, competitive displays, social events, and activities for non collecting spouses.

The ANA was founded in 1891. Its headquarters, research library, and museum are in Colorado Springs, Colorado, adjacent to Colorado College. There are several classes of membership in this organization. These include general membership with annual dues, club memberships for clubs that want to belong to the larger organization, and lifetime membership for very dedicated collectors.

Young Numismatists Organizations

Local, regional, and national organizations often have special activities for young numismatists. This is important if you want to encourage your children to participate in your hobby interests. It is also important if a young member of your family takes an early interest in coin collecting, even if none of the family's adults do.

The ANA is among many coin collecting organizations that hold mock coin auctions and other children's activities during their conventions or meetings. These auctions involve real coins donated by collectors and coin dealers. The YNs purchase the coins by bidding with play money, and they get to keep what they have won.

Learned Societies

Another way to enjoy the social aspect of coin collecting is to join one of the many scholarly coin collecting societies. Coin collecting can be more than the assembling of a group of coins as a hobby pursuit, and it can be more than a way to make money as a business.

Although coin collectors are often referred to as numismatists, a numismatist is a person who studies coins and currency to learn more about society.

CHAPTER 4

-

THE VALUE OF THE COIN

A coin's value, like almost anything's value, is based upon one main factor and only one: what someone is willing to pay for it!

This may seem simplistic, but what are you getting for your money when you think about a rare painting? You get some canvas and paint and a border around it. With a coin, you get a small piece of metal with a date and some images on it.

The value has nothing to do with the date or how old or rare it is; it has nothing to do with what metal it is made of (unless it is gold or the wrong metal) or really what condition it is in. The price it sells for is based upon demand and interest only.

There are very rare coins with low mintage selling for very little money because the interest is not there. I have pennies that are hundreds of years old and very rare but worth very little. On the other hand, a 1943 D copper penny sold for almost 2 million dollars. Why? It is based upon interest.

Collectors want certain types of coins, and the date of mintage and condition are not always critical factors. Concerning the 1943 D copper penny, only one of these coins has ever been found, and this added to its value, but the demand and interest in the coin drove the price up.

The guitar Jimi Hendrix played Star Spangled Banner at Woodstock was auctioned off at $ 1.67 million. It was a white Fender Stratocaster, a very common guitar (except that it was transformed for left handed guitarists). My brother has that exact same model, the same color too, he is very fond of it and he would never think of selling it, but if he did, I'm pretty sure the price wouldn't even get closer to the Jimi Hendrix one. Do you find it strange? I bet you don't.

I am sure you see the point here. I am not saying that condition and rarity are not important; it is. But the main factor is demand. That being said, coin journals that show value are giving you a very rough estimate only. The only way to determine worth is to see what identical coins are selling for.

Let's divide coins into two groups. The first group is for coins that do not have lots of value. The second group is for coins worth thousands. Where is the dividing point here? Is it $500, $1000, $10000. I cannot answer this. If you consider a coin to be very valuable and want to get top dollar for it, you must first determine, among other factors:

- Is the coin real or it is fake?
- Has a reputable grading company verified it?
- What do similar coins sell for?
- Do coins like these sell online at eBay, or do they sell through top auction companies like Heritage?

This process is identical to the one of artwork estimating. First, art is verified. The auction house estimates the value, puts it up for sale, and might set a minimum price before purchasing it. Unless the bidding reaches the minimum, the painting will not be sold to anyone.

When you find a coin that you think to be of value, go online to sites like eBay and see what similar coins are selling for. This is a good starting point. Look closely at the condition and description so you can compare your coin to it.

Then, post pictures of your coin on forums and see what the experts say. Try to determine if the coin is the real error in question and try to determine the condition. Value their opinions but don't take them to the bank. Show it to the local coin club and get their view also. Please do not show it to any local coin stores.

You must have it verified by a major grading company for a coin worth thousands and then sold by a reputable auction house. For one worth hundred, you should sell it yourself. I would not spend any money having a coin graded unless it was worth well over $100.

Dealing with a grading company is a very simple procedure. Most of the labor can be done online, but I prefer calling them first and finding out the procedure for sending a coin for identification and grading. The fee for this is minimal and is necessary. No one will pay for a valuable coin that has not been certified.

Before going to this expense, I suggest you contact the auction houses and find out their policy for submitting a coin for sale. They may have you send the coin to them and have it graded for you. Policies change all the time so call first.

CHAPTER 5

-

HOW AND WHERE TO GET COINS?

I know you are already very excited about actually starting to add coins to your collection, so I am happy to let you know that the time has come for you to learn more about this!

Before we dive into the topic, keep in mind the following ground rules:

- This might seem like a lot of information, but if you approach everything systematically, you have a very good chance to "digest" all these tips and thoroughly follow them.

- Don't rush. As mentioned before, coin collecting is not any kind of race. Acquire your time, work your way up, and be patient. Rome wasn't built in a day, nor great coin collections. Learn to enjoy the hunting process even more than you enjoy the coins themselves…that's when you will truly start to love this activity.

Now that this has been cleared, we proceed with the actual core information you need to know about getting those coins in your collection.

Where to Get Coins?

We have seen how a great way to start out a coin collection is to look into what you may already have. Change in your pocket, coin tray, purse. But once you have figured out this is something you like, you may of course want to take it to a next, more engaging, level.

As a beginner coin collector, you might feel like a basic search on Google opens the doors to a sort of Wild West of collectible coins. Every new search and every new site you open is likely to provide you with a seemingly endless range of options - some of which might sound too good to be true.

As with pretty much all else in life, what sounds too good to be true is most likely not true, and collectible coins sold over the internet will mostly fall in this category.

Indeed, it can be hard to resist temptation when good shiny offers are everywhere, but do keep in mind that educating yourself and researching your potential purchases are key ingredients to doing this successfully.

The beneficial news is that not all internet resources for coin collectors are scams. Many of them are legit, and they will provide you with good opportunities to purchase great coins for your collection.

So, where exactly do collectors buy coins?

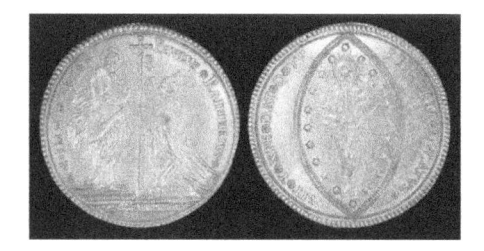

Coin Dealers

The safest way to start collecting coins is coin dealers. However, even in this case, you would still have to make sure you are buying your coins from a reputable coin dealer. Your best bet is to go with dealers who have been approved by the Professional Numismatists' Guild (PNG).

This means that they will adhere to very strict rules regarding the coins they sell and even the prices at which they sell them.

Yes, coin dealers might not seem as attractive an offer as many other sources (including online auctions, as you will see further on). However, they are a safe bet, especially if you are just starting in this.

Third-party certification services also approve some dealers, but it is always good to keep your eyes open regarding these matters. Aside from being a member of PNG, here are some other criteria you should be looking for when selecting your coin dealer:

- Are they experienced? How long have they practiced this?
- Are they specialized in a specific type of coin?
- Do they have any assets? A financially stable coin dealer will usually be less likely to try anything odd, for example.
- Is the coin dealer known among collectors?
- Do they have a good reputation?
- Is there any way you can have recourse if you get tricked into buying something too expensive?

Last but definitely not least, even with a coin dealer, it is still important for you to do your research and solely invest in coins you are certain of. Even more, try not to invest too much from the very beginning.

Most novices start with coins valued between $20 and $100 and work their way up from there–which is precisely what I advise you to do as well.

Online Auctions

Of all the places to buy coins, online auctions can be the most enticing - and for obvious reasons. You can spend hours on end, days, and weeks even searching for coins online, and the internet would serve them up to you on a plate. You don't even have to leave your couch to create a collection that's attractive and valuable. In theory.

In practice, however, online auctions are filled with scams and frauds, so it is even more important to keep your eyes open. A LOT of coin auctions online are perfectly legit, and I encourage you to search your coins on sites like eBay, but it is of the utmost importance to be wary of the potential risks.

As a general rule, only buy from eBay sellers who are reputable and have many reviews. Make sure their coins are graded by a professional from the Professional Coin Grading Service or Numismatic Guaranty Corporation.

Last, but not least, if an offer sounds just too good to be true (i.e., they promise to provide you with a coin that is a lot under the market price), then turn around and run because it is very likely that you are being drawn into a shady auction.

To minimize your risk, start with less valuable coins and only work your way up from there as you gain more experience in both coin collecting and online auctions in general.

Local Coin Shows

Another good way to start collecting coins is by attending local coin shows. Depending on where you live, you might have access to multiple of every year, so you should be able to attend at least one of them.

You can find coin shows on sites like https://coinzip.com/, but do make sure to double-check their authenticity and the dealers who go there. Just because someone sets up a shop at a coin show, it does not necessarily mean that they are truthful all the time - so, as always, keep your eyes open.

One way to select your dealers from a local coin show (aside from the criteria we mentioned before) is by asking them if they have a brick and mortar or permanent online shop as well. If they only attend shows, it is likely that they are either struggling financially (not a good sign) or that they are attempting something shady.

National Coin Shows

Like local coin shows, national coin shows can be a treasure trove of finds for passionate collectors. The same rules apply here as well, though: make sure you stay away from anything that could raise suspicions and only buy from reputable, accredited dealers.

International Conventions

If you are keener on collecting coins from all over the world, there is a very good chance that you will have to attend a few international conventions to make sure you connect to dealers who have coins from outside of the United States as well.

For instance, the New York International Numismatic Convention is a very good source for coins worldwide, if you are interested.

Other Collectors

Another good way to collect coins is by connecting with like-minded people. This will allow you to discuss your interest, learn more, exchange coins, and even buy them from collectors who either have switched their interest or are trying to make a profit.

You can find people with a similar hobby by getting a membership at the American Numismatic Association. You will have to pay for this membership, but the price is quite low (especially compared to the benefits it would offer you).

Also, you can find other coin collectors by joining a local or regional coin club as well. This will allow you to meet up with peers regularly, discuss, and exchange knowledge and coins.

The US Mint

This is perhaps the safest way to make sure your coins are real, valuable, and correctly maintained. However, do keep in mind that the United States Mint might add a pretty steep premium on the coins they put out for sale, so analyze the situation and see if this is worth it for you.

Many collectors wait for a year or two to buy their coins on the secondary markets rather than buy them from the US Mint precisely because the premiums can be very expensive.

Investing In Coin Sets

Another way to invest in coins as a beginner is to set your eyes on coin sets. These are small sets of uncirculated coins released by mints, which can be grabbed at relatively affordable prices. Because they are already grouped, they can feel encouraging and entertaining for new collectors.

Plus, buying these is safer than buying from dealers, shows, or online auctions.

As you can see, there are many sources you can go to when you want to buy coins. As long as you continue vigilant and do not get your heart stolen by shiny coins that might not be of true value, each one of the sources described here can be a gold mine for you.

Tips For Coin Auctions

Regardless of the exact place you choose to buy your coins from, remember that you might often be faced with auctions. Getting to know how to work around these can be daunting when you have never done it before, but a few tips will help:

- Set a maximum bid in your mind. If you are running on a budget (and you definitely should be, no matter how much you can afford to spend on a coin), then set your mind on a specific number not to move past is extremely important. This will help you stay focused, and it will help you withdraw your bid before it is too late for your finances and expectations.

- Consider the buyer's premium and taxes. When setting a budget in mind for your bid, make sure that you also consider the buyer's premium, as well as any kind of taxes you might have to pay for this. Both of these depend on the auction, where it takes place, and where you are located, so you need to check with the legislation in this sense.

- Bid early. The sooner you bid, the more likely it is that you will quickly learn how to get the hang of what is going on and the rhythm of an auction.

- Check your bid. No matter how small your bid may be, and no matter how you choose to place it, make sure your bid reflects your actual intentions.

CHAPTER 6

-

COLLECTIBLE COINS

Suppose you aim to invest purely in gold or silver. In that case, you should buy strictly physical gold and silver bullion coins from national mints or rounds and bars from the major refiners like Engelhard, PAMP, Johnson Matthey, or Credit Suisse. You can also buy junk silver. When I say "physical", I mean gold and silver that you can touch. I'm not talking about paper gold like futures contracts or exchange-traded funds (ETFs).

First, stick to buying your metal from the national mints or the major refiners I mention. These minters and refiners are well-known, and you are less likely to have a buyer who makes you go through the hassle of authenticating your metals when selling.

Keep in mind that the smaller the size, the easier it is to travel with and quickly sell. Finding a buyer for your one-ounce gold American Eagle worth $1200 is usually going to be an easier task than finding a buyer for your 32-ounce gold kilobar worth $40,000.

On the other hand, the larger the bar, the lower the premium you usually pay, so you'll be getting more precious metals for your money.

I wish it were more complicated to explain, but it isn't. It's as simple as that. Here are some forms of gold and silver bullion. And when I mention ounces, I'm referring to troy ounces.

Silver Coins

American Silver Eagles

American Silver Eagles, sometimes known as American Eagle Silver Dollars, were created by the US Mint in 1986. They have an official one-dollar face value and are considered legal tender. Every American Silver Eagle is made from one ounce of .999 fine silver and contains 99.9% silver and 0.1% copper to increase its durability.

American Silver Eagles are shipped from the US Mint in boxes of 500 coins. In each box, you'll find 25 tubes, with each tube containing 20 American Silver Eagles.

Occasionally, backdated or older Silver Eagles can be bought at lower prices than the current year's Silver Eagles.

If you're buying Silver Eagles in bulk, make sure to ask about backdated Silver Eagles before buying the current year's Silver Eagles. American Silver Eagles also have a numismatic value to them.

Also, because these are "legal tender" coins, they are exempt from the IRS form 1099-B reporting requirement. These coins are approved for individual retirement accounts (IRAs). Silver Eagles have high liquidity, which makes them easy to sell. The US Mint frequently sells out of these "three nines fine" coins.

Canadian Silver Maple Leafs

This coin is the Canadian answer to the American Silver Eagle. Canadian Silver Maple Leafs are one-ounce silver coins made by the Royal Canadian Mint and Canada's government starting in 1988. They are legal tender in Canada and are one of the purest silver coins available, containing a super high silver content of 99.99% silver (.9999 fine). Remember, people like us refer to this as "four nines fine" due to the .9999 fine silver content.

They have a radial finish to them that makes the coins almost seem to glow. Maple Leaf has some unique security features like micro-engraved laser markings and anti-counterfeiting technology. Pictures of each coin are taken when they are minted and then encrypted and stored in a database.

Dealers can quickly access this database to check the authenticity of any coin. Although the Maple Leafs have better quality silver, their premiums are usually lower than American Silver Eagles. These coins have high liquidity, are IRS form 1099-B exempt, and can be added to your precious metals IRA.

Junk Silver

For the most part, Junk silver refers to any government coin that contains silver that has zero collectible or numismatic value over the value of the silver it contains. Circulated US coins minted before 1965 are the most popular form of junk silver today. These coins contain 35% to 90% silver and include nickels from 1942-1945, dimes from 1892-1964, quarters from 1892-1964, half dollars from 1916-1969 (Kennedy half dollars from 1965-1969), and dollars from 1878-1935.

You purchase junk silver for its "melt value" or what the coins would be valuable if you liquefied them down and extracted the silver out of them. A $1000 sack (the face value of the pennies in the sack) of US junk silver comprises around 715 ounces of silver.

How do we know this?

At minting, these varieties of coinages had 0.7234 ounces of silver for every face-value dollar. It's agreed that the coins have lost some of their silver due to normal wear and tear over the years. To make up for this loss of silver content, the gold and silver markets have set the standard that 0.715 ounces of silver is now the amount of silver contained in each face dollar of value, which means that a $1000 face value bag of junk silver contains 715 ounces of silver.

You can get a $1000 face value bag of US junk silver for about 1% over the spot price of silver as of this writing. Make sure to keep an eye on the premium you pay per bag, though these coins are sometimes in short supply. When the supply dwindles, dealers charge higher premiums.

The best US junk silver coins to buy are 90% silver, the 1964 Kennedy half dollars, the 1946-1964 Roosevelt dimes, and the 1932-1964 Washington quarters.

Junk silver is not IRA eligible, but IRS forms 1099-B exempt if you are selling less than 715 ounces.

Silver Rounds

Silver rounds are simply coins made by a private mint and not a sovereign state or government, which means they are not legal tender. The main benefit of rounds is that you are paying a lower premium than coins.

Some silver rounds are IRA approved and IRS 1099B exempt if you're selling less than 1000 ounces at a time. These include rounds from Republic Metals Corporation and Sunshine Mint.

Sunshine Buffalo Silver Round

The Buffalo silver round from Sunshine Mint is one of my favorite rounds. It is .999 fine silver and has the same Indian and buffalo images found on American buffalo nickels. Built into the round is a special "MintMark SI" anti-counterfeit technology that allows you to use a special decoder lens to verify the round's authenticity. These silver rounds are IRA approved an IRS form 1099-B exempt if you're selling less than 1000 ounces at a time.

Gold Coins

American Gold Eagles

The United States Mint created the American Gold Eagles in 1986. Unlike the Silver Eagles, Gold Eagles come in four sizes and face values, a $50 face value for the one-ounce coin, a $25 face value for the half-ounce coin, a $15 face value for the quarter ounce coin, and a $5 face value for the tenth-ounce coin. The one-ounce Gold Eagles are the easiest to find, and they contain exactly one troy ounce of gold. American Gold Eagles are 22 karat gold (.916 fine) and contain about 91.6% gold and 8.4% copper-silver alloy.

Remember that this added copper-silver alloy makes the coin more durable and causes all Gold Eagles to weigh a bit more than their stamped gold contents because they still contain one troy ounce of gold in addition to the added metals.

Like the Silver Eagles, Gold Eagles are legal tender but do not sell at their legal tender face value. American Gold Eagles are shipped from the US Mint in boxes of 500 coins. Each box contains 25 tubes, each containing 20 American Gold Eagles. Each box weighs 42 pounds. Dealers will sell these Eagles by the box, the tube, or even the single coin.

Due to their beauty and the experience that they are legal tender, their premium is about 8% to 15% over the spot price of gold, as of this writing.

American Gold Eagles can also have a numismatic value to them. This means some of them can sell for way above their spot and premium price combined, depending on the coin, the condition, and rarity. Also, like the Silver Eagles, because these are "legal tender" coins, do not have to tell the sale to the government when or if you sell them back, unlike some other forms of gold. They are IRS form 1099-B exempt. American Gold Eagles are highly liquid, or easy to trade, and approved for individual retirement accounts.

American Gold Buffalo

In 2006, the US mint created the purest gold coin they have ever offered. Gold Buffalo's contain 24 karats, .9999 fine, or 99.99% gold. Just to beat the lingo into your head a little more, because of this .9999 fine purity, we say the coin has "the four nines" or is "four nines fine".

This is a few of the purest gold coins globally on the level with the gold Canadian Maple Leaf. On one side of the coin, you'll see James Earle Fraser's famous design of an image of American Indian that is also found on old Buffalo Nickels.

On the other side, you'll see an American buffalo, which was a real buffalo so-called Black Diamond, who dwelled in the Central Park Zoo in New York City around the year 1900. These buffalo coins are IRA approved, IRS form 1099-B exempt, and mostly come in one-ounce sizes; although in 2008, the US mint did temporarily create a few other sizes.

Austrian Philharmonic

Although the US American Gold Eagle is the most popular gold coin globally, the gold Austrian Philharmonic coin made by the Austrian Mint has the four nines (.9999 fine) and lower premiums. One side of the coin represents the great pipe organ located in the Golden Vienna Concert Hall. On the other side, you'll find various instruments used in Austria's famous Philharmonic Orchestra. These 24 karat sovereign coins are denominated in Euro. You can add these coins to your precious metals IRA, and they are IRS form 1099-B exempt. They are well recognized around the world.

CHAPTER 7

-

PRESERVE AND PROTECT THE COLLECTION

A cardinal rule for all coin collectors is to avoid causing wear or introducing any substances that may cause spots or color changes.

Try to avoid any direct manual contact with your coins. This means not using your bare hands to handle the coins. Fingerprints are collectible coin's sworn enemies. It is also imperative to make sure that you do not let one-coin touch another coin because it can result in nicks and scratches. To avoid ruining them, remove coins from their storage containers only when needed and necessary.

Uncirculated or Proof coins should not be handled anywhere but the edge, as even a slight fingerprint may reduce its grade and, thus, its value. Proof coins are those struck two or more times with polished dyes on an equally polished planchet; they are legal tender like any regular coins.

Uncirculated mint sets are coins packaged by the US government for sale to coin collectors. It is best if you make it a habit to pick up collectible coins by their edges while wearing clean white cotton or surgical gloves. A face mask is also preferable to prevent small particles of moisture that may cause unwanted spots. Never sneeze or cough near coins because this can leave marks and ruin the coin.

Mint Coins

Coin holders provide enough protection for ordinary handling. If you must take the coin out and need to put it down outside the holder, make sure you place it on a clean and soft surface, preferably a velvet pad. It is an ideal surface and a must-have for handling valuable numismatic materials.

For coins with lesser value, clean, soft cloth may be used. Avoid dragging coins on any surface to avoid scratches. Take note that even wiping with a soft cloth can cause scratches that will reduce its value.

Coin Care And Cleaning

While it is good to maintain cleanliness in the surroundings, it is best not to clean the coins. A shiny coin may look nice, but maintaining its original appearance is essential for a collectible coin.

Cleaning the coin can reduce its numismatic value significantly. There are only a very restricted number of things you can do to improve a coin's appearance. You might harm it instead of enhancing it.

Unnecessary cleaning affects the value and cost of collectible coins. The patina on a coin is built up over the years and is part of its total essence and history, and reflects a value much more than its face value. Remove it, and you can lessen its value by as much as 90%! Collectors value coins with attractive patinas, which, in effect, protect the coin's surface.

Like any work of art restoration, cleaning coins must be done by professionals. They know what techniques to employ that will work best and still have the coin as valuable as ever.

If you think that a tarnished coin you have just discovered needs to be cleaned, STOP! It is not a good idea. It is better to leave the coin alone. The color change you observe is a natural process called toning. And if allowed to progress by itself naturally and produce attractive results, it sometimes adds to the coin's value.

Toning is caused by the atoms' chemical reactions on the coin's surface, usually with sulfur compounds. It cannot be reversed, but "dips" in which strip molecules from the coin's surface are available. Bear in mind, however, that professionals should only do this.

You need to observe several rules when considering cleaning the coins you have obtained, found, bought, or inherited.

1. Never clean a coin that you do not know the numismatic value. If you doubt if it's valuable or not, then don't clean it either. It is best to leave coins the way you found them, untouched. Erring on the

conservative side is preferable than ruining the coin for nothing. Store them in holders made for the purpose. Coin collectors and dealers prefer coins in their original condition, so do not attempt to alter their state. Cleaning will probably ensure more harm than good.

2. Because you are not supposed to clean the coins yourself, you need to take the coins to a professional coin cleaning service. They use a technique called "dipping" that will properly clean the coins without reducing their value. This is important, especially if the coin's date and details cannot be determined because of corrosion. A professional will know how to avoid or minimize further damage to the coin.

3. In the situation that you must clean the coin you have found, then do it with the least harmful method. Do not use harsh chemicals, sulfuric acid, polishing cloth, vinegar, abrasive pastes, or devices that give a smooth and shiny result on the coin. Experiment first with lesser value coins before coins with high value.

4. Cleaning is a big issue in coin collecting, so you have to disclose this fact to a buyer if you are selling a coin that you know has been cleaned.

Soaking coin

Cleaning Different Types Of Coins

- **Uncirculated coins** – should never be cleaned at all because cleaning will ruin any mint luster.
- **Gold Coins** – should be cleansed cautiously in neat, lukewarm bubbly purified liquid consuming a cottony fiber wash-down fabric or an incredibly easy tooth scrub. Gold is smooth metal, so you should take extra care to avoid disfiguring or scratching.
- **Silver Coins** – valuable silver coins should not be cleaned at all. The blue-green or violet oil-like

tarnish, dirt, minerals, or other residue some silver coins have enhanced their appearance and should be left alone. Dark silver coins must be cleaned with ammonia, rubbing alcohol, vinegar, or polish remover with acetone. Do not rub or polish them.

- **Copper Coins** – if necessary to clean, soak them in grape oil. If not available, olive oil will do. Never attempt to rub them in any way. However, getting results may take time, from several weeks to a year, so be patient.

- **Nickel Coins** – best cleaned with warm, soapy distilled water using a soft toothbrush. If cleaning badly stained nickel coins, use ammonia diluted 3 to 1 with distilled water.

How to Store Your Coins

You need to store your coins properly to avoid giving them any scratch to reduce their numismatic value. You need to use the proper type of holder, depending on the value of the coin you are storing.

There are folders and albums available commercially that you can purchase for storing your series or type collection. When using paper envelopes, make sure that their materials are especially suited for holding coins, especially the high-value ones, since sulfur or other chemicals present in the paper can cause a reaction and change the coin's color.

Plastic flips made of mylar and acetate are good materials for long-term storage, but since they are hard and brittle, they may scratch the coin if they are not inserted and removed carefully. "Soft" flips used to be created after polyvinyl chloride (PVC), which decayed after some time and imparted grievous ends aimed at the coinages. PVC gave an emerald look on the pennies. PVC reverses are certainly no longer manufactured and marketed in the US.

Tubes can hold several same size coins and are seemingly for majority space of distributed coinages and higher grade coins if they are not moved. For more valuable coins, use hard plastic holders as they do not contain harmful materials and can protect coins against scratches and other physical damage.

Collectible Coins in their Cases

For more valuable coins, you can opt to use slabs as they offer good protection. Slabs are hermetically sealed hard plastic holders for individual coins. However, one drawback is the expense involved, and you will not be able to get at the coin easily if there is a need to do so.

For long-term storage, a dry environment without significant temperature fluctuation and low humidity are important. You need to minimize exposure to moist air, as this will cause oxidation. It may not reduce the coin's value, but reducing oxidation will help the coin look more attractive. To control atmospheric moisture, you need to place silica gel packets in the coin storage area.

You still need to check on your collection periodically, even if you store them in a safety deposit box. If not stored properly, problems could develop, and you can do something about it before any serious damage occurs.

Protecting Your Collection From Loss By Fire Or Theft

There will always be the threat of loss by fire or theft to any of your properties. However, just as you would protect your house or car from them, there are some precautions you can take to minimize them. Bear in mind that most homeowner insurance excludes coins and other items of numismatic value from coverage. You can usually get a rider, however, but for an additional premium payment.

You can also obtain a separate policy. Consider joining the American Numismatic Association (ANA) that offers insurance for their members' coin collections. Be sure that you have a catalog of your collection stored separately from the coins. Note where you have obtained each coin, the coin's condition, and the price you paid for it.

Taking individual close-up pictures of each coin is also a good idea. Get an appraisal from a professional who uses a Blue Book or Red Book for this purpose. The insurance company will need the documents of the appraisal.

Safes protect against theft, fire, dust, water, or other environmental factors that could damage your possessions. For your coins, they offer relative protection. Some safes provide adequate protection from fire but are not suitable for theft protection.

Some safes do deter thieves but are not fireproof. Your collection can be damaged or destroyed by fire even if the flames do not touch your coins. The heat may be extreme enough to melt them.

Another concern when storing your coins in a safe is the level of humidity. A high level will cause oxidation, which is bad for the coins. The ideal level is 30% relative humidity (RH). The RH inside the safe is dependent on the ambient RH where the safe is located. Most modern safes, fortunately, are adequately insulated and are constructed with good seals. Silica gel packets can help reduce humidity.

So if you opt to keep your collection at home, see that you get a home safe that provides enough fire and humidity protection and protection against theft. Make sure you take measures to prevent or dissuade a burglar from invading your home. Adequate lighting and secure, strong locks are recommended. You can ask law enforcement officers for more valuable tips.

One way of protecting your investment against theft is to be discrete about being a coin collector. The information you divulge about yourself to many people may eventually reach the wrong person. Having all numismatic related promotional materials sent to a post office box instead of your home may help.

CHAPTER 8

-

BUYING COINS

Most collectors and coin hunters will buy coins during their lifetime. Even newbie collectors and hunters purchase coins. Investors often buy coins that will appreciate value over time, and coins made of precious metals, like gold, silver, and platinum, help protect them against economic downturns.

Coins are bought for several reasons: you need a particular coin or coins to complete your collection, you buy coins as gifts, you purchase certain coin sets each year when they are minted (proof or mint sets, for example), you buy precious metal coins hoping they will appreciate over time, you invest in gold coins as part of your portfolio, you purchase a particular coin type each year, buy high grade and rare coins as part of an investment strategy, and the list goes on.

I want to address this topic of buying and investing by listing and explaining the critical components to consider before any purchase:

1. Who do you buy from? Are they dealers you can trust?
2. Are the coins fake or real?
3. What is a fair price?
4. Are coins a good investment?
5. Are high-grade coins worth the price?
6. What websites can be trusted?

Coins can be purchased online (Amazon, eBay, forums and other online venues), or in person at clubs, at shows, from friends, from relatives, at auctions, from dealers, from coin shops, from gold shops, from pawn stores, from grading companies, at estate sales, at yard sales, at swap meets, and on and on.

How do you guard yourself against fraud, and how do you know you are getting a good deal?

There is no simple direction to answer this. You may be at a swap meet and spot an error coin worth thousands, and the vendor is unaware of its value and is asking only $25 for the coin. Should you buy it? Yes, you should. Could it be fake? Yes, it can.

I always recommend spending a certain limit for a coin so that you will not lose any sleep at night, fretting if it turns out to be a fake. For some, that might mean $50, for others $500. It depends upon your financial status. This is an important topic because, well, over 50% of the coins being sold at all venues are fake. These are FBI stats, not mine.

Are there dealers that can be trusted 100% of the time? Yes, there are. All of the grading companies mentioned earlier can be trusted (they sell coins), their certified dealers, and the auction houses. The U.S. Mint can be trusted. Coin clubs are honest, as are certified coin dealers.

What is a certified coin dealer? Several types of certified coin dealers will be mentioned and listed below.

There are many fake-imitators online with names similar to the United States Mint. Be careful.

Most collectors are unaware of the United States Government "Authorized Purchasers" Program. What is it, and how does it apply to me? The United States Mint has created a sales channel for its bullion coins because it does not sell them directly to the public.

They have set up a distribution system with a very limited number of resellers who are trusted and therefore authorized to market their bullion products. Here is some on the list: **Authorized Purchasers of United States Mint Bullion Coins.**

- A-Mark Precious Metals, Inc.
  El Segundo, California 90245
  Silver, Gold, Platinum, Palladium
- American Precious Metals Exchange (APMEX)
  Oklahoma City, Oklahoma 73012
  Silver, Gold, Platinum, Palladium
- Coins & Things, Inc. (CNT)
  Bridgewater, Massachusetts 02324
  Silver, Gold, Platinum, Palladium
- Dillon Gage Inc. of Dallas
  Addison, Texas 75001
  Silver, Gold, Platinum, Palladium
- Fidelitrade, Inc.
  Wilmington, Delaware 19802
  Silver, Gold, Platinum, Palladium

Many of these authorized purchasers (certified dealers) sell directly to the public at rock bottom prices and can be trusted. APMEX, for example, often sells online through popular venues like eBay. Because they buy directly from the United States Mint, it is hard to beat their prices.

However, if you are not in the market for bullion products, the United States Mint lists resellers that carry non-precious metal coins, as well as bullion coins and sets. The United States Mint does not endorse these retailers, but you can have some degree of confidence when buying from them. Please do not confuse them with authorized purchasers. These retailers listed buy bullion from the authorized purchasers, not the U. S. Mint. However, I classify them as certified dealers because they are on the list.

Some coin grading companies mentioned earlier do sell coins directly to the public. Their websites will provide a link to products that are on sale, often found on eBay. However, they also have a list of authorized dealers (again, I refer to them as certified dealers) that they have approved. They provide an honest way to buy coins.

NGC is another grading company that sells coins and has a dealer database (certified) of authorized resellers. Over 1400 dealers are listed.

These authorized dealers (U.S. Mint list and Grading company dealers) have credibility and good history; otherwise, they would not show up on the lists mentioned above. Remember that there are no guarantees in life, but using these directories helps guide you in the right direction.

Coin clubs are a very good avenue to find and buy coins of interest. Members are usually veteran collectors who know the ropes of collecting and often want to get rid of duplicate coins or raise money by selling parts or all of their collection. If you are in the right place at the right time, you will hit the jackpot. That's why getting to know your fellow club members is in your best interest. The chances of getting cheated are very low.

Local pawn and gold-coin shops cannot be trusted. Yes, some are honest, but how do you know which ones are? One of the best studies on their integrity was done some years ago when a coin expert took a valuable coin to over 12 shops and asked them what they thought the value was. The coin was worth over $2500. Virtually all of them misled him, and some even suggested the coin was a fake. Most of them were willing to pay $200.

Buying coins online from local postings, like Facebook and Craigslist, can be problematic.

While the seller may be honest, you have no way of knowing if the coins are real. If the story behind the sale seems credible, you can take a chance. Here's how I handle these situations. If I come across coins I am interested in; such as from a local ad, I always ask the seller if I can send one coin in for certification. If they say no, then you know they are lying about the coins. If they say yes, I take the most valuable coin and send it in for appraisal to determine if it is real.

One last general advice: be choosy and be prepared. Make sure the coin you buy is what you want and need.

This may sound obvious, but believe me, it is not. What I'm going to tell you now falls in the mistake column and is way more common than you think. You can ask anyone who has some history in coin collecting, they all will have some kind of "horror stories" to tell.

Sometimes at a coin show, you have looked at so many coins trying to find what you want that you end up buying the wrong coin by mistake.

For example, you are looking for an 1896 Dollar. You have looked and looked, and finally, you found one at the right price and grade, and you buy it. That is great until you get home and find that you bought an 1886 Dollar instead of the wrong mint.

Another even more common mistake is: you are looking for a 1916S VG penny, and you get home and find out that you bought a 1916D. Trust me; it can happen, so double-check that the coin is what you need and want before buying it.

Sometimes you buy the right coin that you had on your list, and when you get home, you find that you already had that one. It can happen to the best of us. Be certain that your records are up to date before you go shopping.

An old carpenter saying holds here: "Measure twice and cut once or measure once and cut twice." Or in coin collecting terms, check your list twice and the coin twice or check them once and buy the wrong coin.

CHAPTER 9

-

MONETIZING YOUR HOBBY

Whether you started your coin collection as a hobby or as an investment, there will come a time when you will consider selling the coins you have accumulated. You might need to because of a personal financial need or perhaps help out a relative or a friend.

For sure, you will not sell them because you have gone tired of them and have lost interest. And just like any commodity, you expect a fair price to be offered for them, and you also expect to profit somehow from the sale, no matter how small it will be. What you want is to get the most money for your coins as quickly and conveniently as possible.

You have several selections when it comes to selling your collection. You can choose to go by the route of a public auction. Most auction houses, however, have a minimum consignment value. And if yours is below this figure, they will not accept your collection. You will then need to find another dealer who will accept lesser value coins and can auction them for you quickly.

Coins Public Auction

Another way to sell your collection is through a personal sale. This can be the quickest way but could also be the riskiest and time-consuming. You have to approach several dealers and offer your coins for sale. You may or may not partake luck in finding one who can quote a reasonable price for them.

You can also put an ad in the papers, but some of the offers you get through them could be of dubious character. It might be too tardy for you if the offer comes from a dishonest person out to take advantage of people like you.

A third way you could choose is to have your coins consigned to a local dealer. But you should simply do this if you have personal knowledge of the dealer's background. Ask the dealer if they are willing to accept the coins for a certain amount to impose a markup. Most dealers will accept this since they have no financial investment as the markup is already a sure profit.

For our reasons here, we will discuss the second option: personal sales.

The first thing you need to do is know exactly what you have in your collection and how valuable it is to you, the dealer, and the buyers. You need to know what you will be selling so you need to do some homework.

The first duty you have to accomplish is to create an inventory of all your collection. You need to identify each coin to know how much each is worth and how much your entire collection is worth. You may already have an idea, especially if you have purchased all of them.

You might even think that based on your calculations of the price you paid when you acquired them plus a markup, you would be making a handsome profit, right?

Besides, if you have been reading coin-value magazines, you know that a certain coin in your collection is worth this much. Well, it depends. Remember that the price you paid when you bought your coins and the price listed on those magazines are retail prices and not what a dealer would pay. Also, a lot of the value depends on the collection's condition. They would have to be checked for damage. The bottom line is, you will not receive what you expect, and it will be a lower amount.

You can also refer to one of the references mentioned above, the "*Official Red Book: A Guide Book of United States*

Coins". It can give you an idea of the approximate range of value of your coins.

Now you need to find a dealer who can appraise your coins correctly. Do some research and look at the background of several dealers you have in mind. You can find them at the website of the Professional Numismatic Guild (PNG). It would help you that the dealers are reputable members in good standing of the American Numismatic Association (ANA) or any known numismatic club. You may have to learn it the hard way, but at this point, you have to make sure that the dealer you will finally choose is honest and will give you what your coins are worth.

Once you have made your choice, take steps to contact the dealer. You can do this either by phone or email if they have one. When you contact them, identify yourself, inform them about your intention to sell your collection, and give them the inventory list you created earlier. If you are in luck, the dealer may accept your collection. If not, and the dealer is not interested in your collection because it is an average one and will not profit from it, you just need to go to the next dealer on your list.

The dealer who accepts your collection will make an offer, which could sound very disappointing to you. The dealer will most certainly not offer the price you were expecting but rather the wholesale price, which is much lesser than the retail price.

Remember that the price you had in mind is the retail price, the amount you are willing to pay for the coins. The dealer will give you the price that he will pay so that he or she can profit when your collection is sold. Besides, the dealer reserves the right to revise the offer based on the coins' actual condition.

The dealer may not agree with the grade of the coins you had in mind and if the dealers are lower, expect a huge drop in the price offered. If, for one reason or another, you couldn't agree on a price that's reasonable to both of you, go to the next dealer on your list again.

At one point in your search for the right dealer, you may want to consider offering your collection to an auction house. If your collection meets their criteria, you may be able to get a higher price. However, make sure you are mindful of the fees involved and do some math. You may or may not come out the winner in this case.

The Finer Points Of Selling Your Collection

To better understand what has been discussed above, a closer look at the world of coin dealers is in order.

Coin dealers come in two categories. There are the wholesaler and the retailer. The wholesaler is the one who seeks out new coins to bring into the marketplace. To do this, this type of dealer attends coin shows, auctions, and some may even run advertisements to buy coins. Since this dealer sells the coins' wholesale, you can expect them to have a lower price. But as a coin collector, you can't just go to these dealers and buy from them. You go to the retailers to buy your coins.

The retailers usually get the bulk of their coins from the wholesalers. They also attend coin shows, auctions, etc. Their primary customers who bring them the money are the ordinary single coin buyers looking to start or complete their collection.

Wholesale Coin Prices

Whether you are selling or buying coins, knowing the wholesale prices of coins will help you transact with any dealer type. This information can be obtained from the Coin Dealer Newsletter, more commonly known as the "Grey Sheet." This publication lists the "bid" and "ask" prices for every important US coin. "Bid" price refers to what dealers will pay another dealer for coins. "Ask" price refers to what dealers ask to buy or what they want their clients to pay them, which is usually higher than the bid price.

When you call a dealer to buy coins. The dealer will quote you the "ask" price. But when you call to sell coins, the dealer will quote you the "bid" price, again usually lower than the "ask" price. This is how dealers make money, just like with any other commodity: buy low, sell high.

Bear in mind, though, that these transactions are about wholesale selling, which means bulk orders and no single coins. Deals like this require a minimum quantity of coins to work. Do not expect dealers to pay you the "bid" prices listed in the Grey Sheet. This publication gives you enough ideas, so you don't sell your collection worth $10,000 for $500. A lot of dealers would like that.

Another point to consider about wholesale coin pricing is that the more valuable the coin is, the smaller the profit margin will be in terms of percentage. For example, a coin that sells for $10,000 can be bought by a dealer for $9,000. The dealer is sure to make a handsome profit if it is sold at the original price. However, the dealer's investment is left tied up and the coin stuck in the inventory for a long time before a coin buyer can develop the $10,000, a hefty amount.

Two Ways To Sell Your Coin Collection

There are two ways you can sell your collection, whether it is a complete set or a random collection of types or series. You can sell them as a complete set or sell them as individual coins. Each way has its advantages and disadvantages. It depends on how much effort you can give to each task.

You can sell your coin collection as a complete set, but this way, you may not get the money you expect from each coin, although you can be sure that you can sell the whole lot. If you have a complete set to sell, the best way to do it is to leave them as they are. It is important to know what they are worth.

Compare what you know to be reasonable with the bids you will receive, whether it's close to the figure you have or way below. It might be low but consider the work you would save if you have to sell the coins individually.

Selling the entire collection may be the least time consuming and least labor-intensive way to sell them.

You can then bring them to the dealer or coin shop of your choice with an inventory so they can check your collection easily.

You can also opt to sell cone coins and make some more money from each coin. However, you can expect some coins to be left behind, especially the ones with lesser value.

Selling one coin at a time involves so much effort than selling the entire collection at once. Thus, you must find the balance between what you hope to receive for the entire collection against what you will potentially earn if you sell them as individual coins. Remember that you need to put many hours and leg work to sell them individually.

Do not lower your prices until you exhaust all possibilities of getting a higher price and are sure no one else will buy your coins at your asking price. Your best bet is to concentrate on getting high bids for your highest value coins.

CHAPTER 10

-

ANATOMY OF A COIN

Refined metal is usually shipped in the form of ingots. These are large, rectangular metal blocks, which can range from an ounce to hundreds of ounces. When you see pictures of Fort Knox, the bricks of gold pictured in the vaults are ingots.

The ingots are rolled out into strips at the mint by passing through rolling machines, much like rolling out the dough in a pasta maker. Each pass through the rolling machine will stretch it out further, and each time through the machine, the rollers are adjusted to give a narrower tolerance until the ingot has been rolled out to the thickness of the coin.

After being rolled into strips, the metal is sent to the punching machine. This machine will punch circles out of the metal. These circles are approximately coin-sized and are called blanks. Blanks must be marginally smaller in diameter and thicker than the final product because the blank will be "squeezed" during the minting process. The pressure will force the metal to take the shape of the coin.

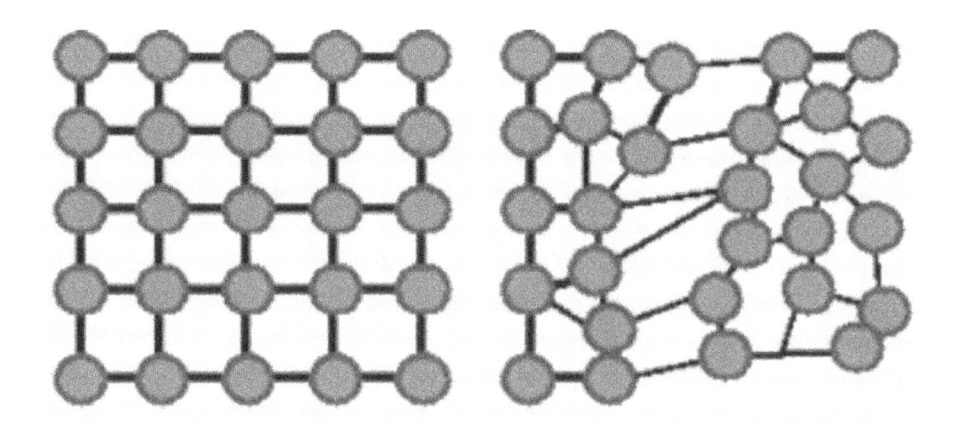

All of this rolling and stretching affects the internal molecular structure of the metal. The atoms of metal form a three-dimensional structure that is rearranged by all of this stress. A perfect structure would have the atoms aligned in neat rows and columns, as seen in the left structure in the figure above, but the work hardening breaks the bonds between the atoms and forms dislocations. These dislocations resist any further stress and form an irregular pattern, as you can see in the figure above.

This problem is solved by a process called "annealing." The blanks are placed in a furnace and heated to a certain temperature (the US mint uses temperatures above 700 C). When heated, the atomic bonds can reform back to their regular structure. If allowed to cool to room temperature slowly, iron will be much softer.

Following the annealing process, blanks are run through the "upsetting mill," which tumbles them until a raised lip is formed around the coin's edge. This raised lip will help direct the flow of metal later in the minting process and be the coin's highest point. This will become the rim, which helps protect the central designs. After the raised lip is formed, the blanks are called planchets and are delivered to the coining room.

There are three dies required to make a coin – each die corresponds to one side of the coin. The front of a coin is usually considered to be the side with the date. Traditionally on American coins, this has been the side with the bust of a historical figure or an image of Lady Liberty. The front of a coin is called the "obverse." The back of a coin is called the "reverse." On American coins, the reverse has traditionally had an eagle image, a statement of value, or a wreath design of some sort.

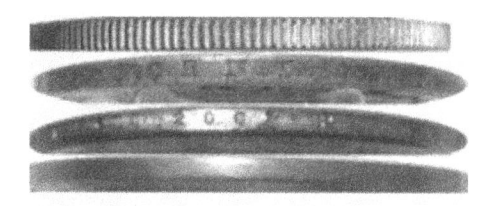

The third side of a coin, the edge, is often ignored. The edge is usually smooth on lower denominations, as seen in the bottom picture in the figure above (called "plain"). Higher denominations traditionally made of silver or gold have reeded edges (the top picture in Figure above). The reeded edge was originally an anti-fraud device to deter "clipping." Crooks would take silver or gold coins and shave slivers of metal off the edge and return the coin to circulation at full face value. They would accumulate the slivers of metal and sell them as scrap, profiting from the difference. The coins would thus weigh less than they were supposed to.

Various terms are used to describe the parts of a coin's design. The raised designs are called the devices – the eagle, bust, wreath, letters, or other items on the coin.

The amount that the devices are raised is the "relief" of the coin. The lower parts of the coin (which look like blank space) are called the fields. The obverse of a Franklin half a dollar is pictured in Figure above. The devices of this coin are white, and the fields are black.

Fields are not usually perfectly flat – they have a curvature to them. This curvature helps direct the flow of metal during striking and accentuates the relief of the devices. The amount of curvature is called "basing." Some coins have a much higher curvature than others – the Mercury Dime has more base than the Roosevelt dime.

Around the edge of the coin, both obverse and reverse is a raised rim. The rim begins as the upset edge before striking and becomes a flat raised border after striking. Raised rims help protect the inner designs of the coin from wear or damage during the life of the coin. They are also important in being able to stack coins – the uniform height around the coin provides a level stacking surface.

Certain classic coin designs were struck without rims and proved very susceptible to damage. The rim also serves to frame the design of the coin artistically. In the figure above, you can see the dentils from a Capped Bust Half dollar at left. These dentils were hand punched into each die, so there are variations in the dentils' size and shape around the coin. On the right, you can see the dentils from a Morgan Dollar. These were created by machines and had a much more regular appearance.

A very important feature of coins is the mintmark. This is a small letter or symbol that identifies where the coin was struck. In the US, the mintmark is a letter identifying the mint; England, France, and many other countries use "privy marks" to identify the mint. The mint mark originated in ancient times when the amount of money a coin was worth was based on its metal content. If underweight coins were found, or coins with less pure metal, it would be easy to track which mint was causing the problem.

The mintmark can be on any part of the coin. Most modern coins have the mintmark on the obverse close to the date, as you can see on the Lincoln Cent in the figure above.

BONUS CHAPTER

-

BUYING COINS: SAFETY UPDATE

SCAM ALERT

We already had this topic covered in chapter 8 "Buying Coins". However, on this new edition I thought that was a good idea to give some new and updated information about the safety side of buying coins, particularly addressing how to avoid scams (online and offline)

Here's a big deal; a large percentage of coin purchases involve fake coins. Also, when bought online, coins that are shipped often do not correspond to their description on the website. And if you are not savvy enough if the coin you receive is not the coin described, you may not spot the difference.

Did you know that the United States FBI has become involved in fake coins because over 50% of the coins sold online are fake? It is such a big business that people are scammed out of millions of dollars each year, and in many cases even certified and encapsulated coins, are fake.

There is a mass-production of coins that are completely or partially fake. Some of the most common cases are:

- Coins are altered
- Coin grading is faked
- Dealers sell real coins and fake coins at the same time
- Dealers sell coins that are not the coins being displayed
- Dealers sell coins that have been altered and may not know about it
- Dealers sell fake coins and may not know about it

No worries. Here is how to protect yourself. If you are new to coin buying, there are two important points to keep in mind.

Point one: unless you are super confident of what you are doing, always spend little money on a coin. Chances are that a coin priced $25 or less is not fake. If you need a coin or two to complete a collection, and the coins you want to buy are inexpensive, the chances of being taken advantage of are small, and even if you should get conned, you wouldn't lose too much money.

Point two. Never buy rolls of coins online. Never!

What's up with online moved coins? Probably the best article ever composed regarding this matter ought to be rehashed. Kindly read it cautiously: Buying Unsearched Rolls.

"At some random time, eBay has two or three hundred closeouts for unsearched rolls. The new prevailing fashion on eBay is bank wrapped moves demonstrating a key or semi-key date on end, and the old trend is highlighting their (the seller's) criticism on the number of key dates that have been found in the moves they are selling.

Most coins found in bank wrapped rolls are normal and all-around flowed coins. Shotgun wrapped rolls can be opened, looked at that point re-pleated as though it originated from a bank. Similar rolls can be looked at and a key date put on the end, at that point, re-pleated as unsearched.

For instance, suppose I have a shotgun move of Lincoln Wheat Cents, and all are normal dates. Along these lines, I purchase a 1909-S key date for $125 (this is the real book estimation of the coin in great condition), and I supplant the end coin with the 1909-S Lincoln. Additionally, I realize that a 1909-S with the VDB on the back is worth $900, and I likewise realize that you can't check whether the 1909-S toward the finish of the re-pleated roll has a VDB or not. Presently I start my sale on eBay with an *announcement "Unsearched shotgun move with a 1909-S appearing" and an inquiry, "Is this a 1909-S VDB?".*

I kick back and watch my $125 venture sell for over $255.00 because a few purchasers needed to hazard the opportunity to find a 1909-S VDB. In this way, they pay $130 more than the roll is worth, and my PayPal account develops over a hundred dollars more. Presently I'm thinking, " What if I did this with ten rolls? I could make well over 1,000 dollars in a week!" To top it all off, other eBay sellers see my success and copy my act. Now, it's a huge problem."

Now you know how easy it is to fake a roll, and most rolls online are fake. No one is going to sell an unsearched roll. All rolls have been searched and repackaged. In case you are wondering, a shotgun roll is a roll wrapped by a machine that makes the roll look like it has never been opened – tightly sealed.

If you want to spend more than $25 on a coin, it is advisable to do this safely. Having an in-depth understanding of how coins are faked and who to buy coins will help make wise decisions.

Let's start by looking at the fake coin topic to understand the magnitude of the problem. Many foreign countries have large factories, whose only mission is to produce fake United States coins. They make fake silver dollars and produce gold coins that contain real gold (but are not legitimate U.S. currency), fake old coins, and the list goes on.

These fakes are sold to resellers who list them online, claiming they are real, and most buyers are happy with the purchase because the coin looks legitimate, and the buyer can't tell the difference. To make matters worse, the seller's feedback may be 100%, yet many of the coins they are selling are fake!

Chinese made fake silver dollars "Morgan". The easiest way to spot a fake coin is just by looking at it. Most fakes look perfect, no ware, almost plastic-like, hot off the press.

Many fakes do not weigh the same as the real version or are attracted to a magnet because of their metal content.

These Chinese made silver dollars look perfect and are probably made from cheap metal. If you weigh them, and I guess that they will not be the correct weight of 26.73 grams, they might be magnetic. Testing to see if they have a magnetic pull can help determine validity. Cheap metals often stick to a magnet. However, some fake coins have the correct weight and are not magnetic!

Many coins being sold online have been altered, and it is very hard to spot this if you are not trained in this subject. Most coin collectors are not.

I mentioned earlier that even certification had been faked. The major coin grading companies written about earlier have developed a grading validation service on their websites, and in some cases, an app you can use on your phone.

This allows you to enter the coin number found on the case and compare it to the grading company records to verify its integrity. This helps protect your purchase. It allows you to check an encapsulated coin before you even buy, so you are not cheated.

I have established over the years that buying from reputable dealers is probably your best option that makes the buying experience a valid one. Finding a reputable dealer is fairly easy.

Buy from the auction companies listed earlier, buy coins listed on the grading company websites, and only buy from certified dealers. As we have seen previously, the U.S. Mint allows certain coin companies to become certified. It is a very expensive process, and the U.S. Mint accepts only a limited number of coin sellers into their dealership program. While these dealers focus on bullion type sales, they also sell other types of coins.

Unfortunately, many coin collectors end up buying from eBay and other similar sites, which leads to trouble. Many online sellers are honest, but so many are not that it is very hard to know if you are trading with someone reputable. Remember, the FBI states that over 50% of online coin sales involve fake coins.

Please look for these red flags: (It does not mean the seller is bad. Please proceed with caution before buying from them.)

Dealers that sell certified coins and coins that are not certified. They certify some coins to create the impression that they only sell a good quality product.

- Always check the feedback carefully. However, some dishonest sellers have a 100 % positive rating.

Many of these coins are fake.

- Dealers that always have a very large supply of high-quality coins for sale.

- Dealers have rare coins on sale that are in perfect condition and priced very low.
- Dealers do not claim that the picture of the coin is the actual coin you will receive. They bait and switch.
- Dealers that do not have a good return policy.
- Coin pictures are not clear and detailed and only show the front of the coin.

Here's the bottom line. Only buy certified coins, and check the certification, if you are spending over $75 on a coin. Never pay more than this for a coin that has not been certified! If buying a set of coins, make sure you can return the set if not satisfied.

Once you receive the set, have at least one of the better coins certified.

CONCLUSION

People collect coins for all sorts of reasons. Someone to take a virtual tour of the historical route of a country. Someone may be fascinated by the journey any coin has had, passing by the hands and through the lives of countless individuals who lived decades, even centuries back. Virtually anyone could have been in contact with that very coin, even celebrities or historical figures.

Someone else is just fascinated by the idea of collecting something that is of very common use but at the same time could be incredibly valuable, maybe without most people even can tell. And they like to be ones to know this hidden in plain sight secrets.

And for some other people it could just be having a fun and exciting pastime that can also be a medium/long term investment. A treasure that you can grow little by little, day by day, with no great expense at the beginning, and then end up with a valuable collection that is worth way more than the single parts as you collected them during the path.

Whatever may be your reason or motive, whether it's one among the above ones, or another one absolutely personal and peculiar, I hope this book could have help you in finding a way to start and some hint to move confidently your first steps into this wonderful journey.

Then, of course, I wish that this will be the first book of many, and that it would have just sow the seed of a new passion in you